COMMUNICATION
SNACKS

52 BITE-SIZED COMMUNICATION TIPS
FOR THE BUSY PROFESSIONAL

Marc J. Musteric & Blythe J. Musteric

Communication Snacks:
52 Bite-Sized Communication Tips for the Busy Professional

Marc J. Musteric & Blythe J. Musteric

© 2016 Ovient, Inc.

Ovient, Inc.
440 Wolfe Road
Sunnyvale, CA 94085

Visit our website at www.ovient.com.

Library of Congress Control Number: 2016920026

ISBN-13: 978-0-9894305-1-7

Printed in the United States of America

Cover & book design by: Stuart L. Silberman
Editing by: Allison B. Tubio

First Edition: December 2016

Contents

Set a Communication Goal for the Next 52 Weeks 1

How to Sound Confident...3

Keep a Conversation Going...5

Effective Presentations Start at Zero.................................7

Overcome Writer's Block at Work......................................9

Respond to Questions When You Don't Have an Answer.... 11

Lead Effective Meetings...13

Commonly Confused Words That Sound the Same...........15

How to Handle Criticism..17

Command Attention Through Silence..............................19

The Presentation Strike Zone...21

How to Really Listen...23

Two Must-Haves for Every Effective Presentation 25

Project Confidence When Saying Your Own Name...........27

Acronyms and Initialisms 29

Give Up Control for More Polite Communication 31

Master Email Etiquette..33

Who Is Responsible for Communication? 35

Clarify Your Points with Speech Capsules........................37

Quotation Marks with Commas, Periods,
and Question Marks 39

Magnetic Eyes Show Confidence 41

Small Talk Matters 43

I or *Me*? 45

The Short-Answer, Long-Answer Response 47

How to Use a Dash 49

Soften Statements by Avoiding *You* 51

Avoid the Coffee Stain Problem When Presenting 53

It's or *Its*? 55

Is It Time for a Communication Reboot? 57

Give to Get 59

How to Use a Semicolon 61

Present Your Ideas Positively 63

So, Like, Um, Yeah, You Know 65

Word Count and Culture 67

How to Use *Etc.* Correctly 69

Recover Quickly 71

How to Avoid Talking Too Much 73

Two Kinds of Presentation Pauses 75

Understand and Use Hyphens 77

How to Present to Executives 79

Avoid Misunderstandings Before They Happen 81

Give Your Presentation Bookends 83

How to Soften a Question 85

Avoid Absolutes 87

How to Use a Colon...89

Acknowledge Beliefs and Perceptions.............................91

How to Present Effectively from a Seated Position...........93

Count to Five After Asking Questions............................95

How to Use *E.g.* and *I.e.* Correctly 97

When to Use *Save Draft*..99

Measure Actions, Not Confidence...............................101

Condense Your Message in a Pinch 103

Index...105

Introduction

When I was 16 years old, I accidentally dropped a large table on a BMW. I was carrying the table through a hotel parking lot as part of my summer job. I lost my balance and dropped the table. It broke the BMW's side mirror clean off. I immediately knew I had made a huge mistake. The rest of that day was tough, but I apologized, I got through the day, and I kept my job.

Sometimes communication is like this. You make a big mistake, but you know what you've done wrong. You apologize, and you move on. Often, however, communication mistakes are not so obvious. Was your presentation really that great, or was the audience just being polite? Was the email you sent offensive? Did you use that semicolon correctly? Even when you recognize that you've made a communication mistake, you may not know how to fix it. This can be a big problem.

As you progress in your career from entry level employee to manager to executive, communication becomes increasingly important. Your success depends on your ability to persuade, build consensus, and inspire. It also depends on your ability to quickly recognize your communication mistakes and correct them.

We wrote this book for you, the busy professional. It covers key areas of communication, including interpersonal communication, intercultural communication, grammar, and presentations. The goal is to give you tips for communicating more effectively and show you how to avoid making serious communication mistakes. We call these tips **Communication Snacks**. Think of them as your communication nourishment for the next 52 weeks. If you feed your communication skills, they will grow, develop, and improve, and you will grow professionally as a result.

How to Use This Book

Each Communication Snack is a single bite-sized tip, just one or two pages long, written in practical, easy-to-digest language. The tips move fluidly (and somewhat randomly) between various communication topics. This is on purpose. We want you to experience the tips much like you experience communication in your daily life. We also want you to be a bit surprised (and delighted) as you move through the book and explore the tips. (Of course, if you are looking for tips on a specific topic, you can always take a look at the topic index on page 105.) We hope you will pick up the book once a week, read a Communication Snack, and spend a few minutes thinking about how you might apply that tip to your work.

For more than ten years, we have been helping professionals in Silicon Valley communicate with one another. Thousands of people move here every year from around the US and around the world. As a result, Silicon Valley is a rapidly changing sea of cultures, concepts, and connections. These 52 Communication Snacks have helped our clients sort through the frequent miscommunications that occur in this dynamic, multicultural Silicon Valley ecosystem. Some of our clients have carried these tips with them to the highest levels of the executive suite. We hope you like them too. Happy snacking!

Marc J. Musteric and Blythe J. Musteric

1

Set a Communication Goal for the Next 52 Weeks

Improving your communication skills can be tricky. Why not start by setting a communication improvement goal? Ask yourself these two questions:

1. **What is one area or situation where I feel uncomfortable or inarticulate when communicating?**

2. **How would my life or career be better if I could communicate more effectively in this situation?**

By answering these questions, you will (1) identify an area where you need improvement and (2) find a source of motivation by connecting your goal with positive changes in your life or career.

As you read through these Communication Snacks over the next 52 weeks, think about how they relate to your goal. If you would like to attack your goal more directly, take a look at the topic index on page 105. This index should help you identify which Communication Snacks will help you reach your goal.

2

How to Sound Confident

Sounding confident involves being mindful of your voice. Focus on your voice as if it were the only tool you had to get your message across. The following techniques will help you use your voice effectively and confidently:

Control Your Voice

Before you speak, relax your voice by taking a few deep breaths, counting to three as you exhale slowly. When you speak, choose the appropriate volume for your room size.

Use Falling Intonation

To make convincing statements, your intonation (voice pitch) should fall at the ends of your sentences. A rising voice pitch sounds uncertain.

Slow Down

Many speakers speak too quickly during speeches and presentations. It is natural to speed up when you are nervous, so be careful! Write "SLOW DOWN" in your notes or tell someone in the audience to motion to you if you are speaking too quickly.

Speak in Full Sentences

It is easy for your mind to start moving faster than your mouth. Be patient and allow yourself to complete your sentences before moving on to the next thought. Completing your sentences will help you stay focused on your topic.

Tip: Record yourself giving a speech or presentation. Listen to the recording. Do you hear confidence in your voice? If not, practice until you are satisfied with the way you sound.

3

Keep a Conversation Going

Getting to know people through small talk is extremely important for making and maintaining connections. Keeping the conversation going can be a challenge, though, especially when you don't know much about the topic being discussed. If you sometimes find yourself not knowing what to say, think of the acronym **ACE:** *Ask, Connect, Expand*.

If you don't know much about the topic, *ask* "W" and "H" questions (who, what, where, when, and how).

> Where are they located?
>
> How does that process work?

If you have some personal experience with the topic, **connect** your experience with the topic.

> I went there last year.
>
> I once participated in a workshop that they offered.

If you happen to know a little bit about the topic, you can **expand** the topic.

I heard on the news that they're hiring.
I read that they redesigned their logo.

4

Effective Presentations Start at Zero

How can you maintain composure and confidence when presenting or speaking in public? Find and master your Zero Position.

The **Zero Position** is the position of your body when you start a speech or presentation and the position you return to when you are between gestures. This is your ready position. Everything you do during your presentation or speech should start from and return to this position.

The Zero Position is a concept taken from athletics. From karate to dance, most coordinated physical activities incorporate the idea of a preparatory posture. The purpose of the Zero Position is to coordinate your mind and body and prepare both for what comes next.

When speaking in public or presenting, the Zero Position can help you project confidence and control nerves. By returning to the Zero Position when you are nervous, you will avoid doing things that make you look nervous, such as swaying back and forth, adjusting your shirt, or playing with a ring or necklace.

Finding Your Zero Position

To find your Zero Position, stand in front of a mirror with your shoulders back. Open your feet slightly into a "V" position, with one foot slightly in front of the other and your weight on the back foot. Place your hands together just above your waistline and slightly away from your body. You should look and feel comfortable and grounded.

If this position is not quite comfortable for you, try varying it a bit. You can drop one hand to your side while keeping the other just above your waist, for example. Just make sure your Zero Position has these three elements: You should have at least one hand slightly above your waist, your feet should be slightly apart, and your weight should be slightly more supported by the rear foot.

When you begin your next presentation, walk confidently to the front of the room. Find your Zero Position and pause for 1-2 seconds before you begin. You will feel in control and you will look confident.

5

Overcome Writer's Block at Work

You are writing a report, proposal, email, blog post, or press release, and you get stuck. You cannot seem to get your ideas down on paper. You find yourself writing and rewriting the same sentence multiple times.

You've just experienced writer's block.

Fortunately, there are easy ways to overcome writer's block at work. Next time you are stuck, try one of the following strategies:

1. **Simplify your language.** It is easy to get stuck trying to create a "perfect" or "elegant" sentence. Keep your sentences short and simple. Avoid unnecessary connectors, wordy phrases, and complex clauses. Imagine you have only 140 characters to say what you are trying to say. Constraints will help you leave out unnecessary words and phrases.

2. **Say it aloud.** Imagine that you are talking to the person who will be reading your writing. Try saying your

sentence aloud to get the language out of your head and into the room.

3. Consider another voice. If the words are not flowing from your mind, try writing with another person's voice in your head. How would that person say it? The change in perspective may help you think differently about the sentence.

4. Don't try to write perfect sentences the first time. Try writing whatever comes to your mind first, even if it is written poorly. Once your thoughts are down on paper, go back and revise what you have written.

Tip: If you try all of these strategies and you still cannot get your thoughts on paper, take a 10-minute break. Sometimes your mind just needs to rest.

6

Respond to Questions When You Don't Have an Answer

Imagine this situation: You have just finished your presentation. A hand shoots up. You feel the blood beginning to drain from your face as you listen to the audience member's question and realize you don't have a great answer. What do you do?

Don't panic!

At one time or another most presenters are asked a question they cannot answer. Fortunately, there are several strategies you can use when this happens to you. Here are a few you can try:

1. **Tell the audience member you will get back to them.** You can simply say, "I don't have an answer for you right at this moment, but let me look into that and get back to you."

2. **Respond with what you know.** If you can partially answer a question, you can say, for example, "I don't have a full answer right now, but what I can say is…"

3. Ask the audience. Before you provide an answer, give the other members of the audience a chance to respond. You can say, "That's a great question. Before I respond, does anyone else have a response?" At the very least, you will buy yourself time to consider your answer before speaking. It is also likely that your audience will come up with a great answer for you.

If none of these strategies work, you can always say, "I don't know." This is often a better solution than giving an incorrect answer. In particular, if the question is outside of your area of expertise, it is perfectly normal to admit that you don't have an answer.

Tip: The best way to avoid questions you cannot answer is to prepare! Before your presentation, challenge yourself to write 20 questions your audience might ask you. If you come up with answers before your presentation, you may never need these strategies.

7

Lead Effective Meetings

Leading an effective meeting is like taking your family on a road trip. Just imagine that your road trip destination is your meeting goal and your family is your team, and then follow these five rules:

1. **Clarify your destination.** Make sure everyone understands the destination. If everyone is on the same page, it will be easier to stay focused throughout the meeting. Tell them the goal at the beginning of the meeting: "Today, our goal is to _____."

2. **Keep your eyes on the road.** Once you start, stay focused on the destination. If your group wants to take a detour and discuss an unrelated topic, try to get them back on track as quickly as possible. Some detours are necessary, but too many detours can ruin the trip. You can use phrases such as these: "I know these details are important, but I want to make sure we stay focused on our goal for today" or "It seems like we have gotten off topic. Let's get back to our discussion about _____."

3. **Change drivers with caution.** If you change drivers, plan to do so in advance and do it safely. In our metaphor, the

driver is the leader of the meeting. It is okay to change drivers, but be sure to do it when there is a natural stopping point or topic shift in the discussion: "Lisa will lead us through the discussion of the next section about implementation." It helps to coordinate who will lead (drive) each section of the meeting before the meeting.

4. **Watch the clock and your gas tank.** To reach your destination on time, you will need to keep an eye on the clock. Keep the discussion moving forward. If you get stuck on a minor issue, skip it and go to the next topic.

   In our metaphor, your gas tank represents your group's energy level. Don't expect your team to stay alert and focused for a four-hour meeting. Keep your meetings brief. If you need to have a long meeting, take frequent breaks for refueling.

5. **Capture memories.** Don't forget to capture your memories. If you are on a family trip, you will naturally take a lot of pictures to capture your memories. A meeting is similar. You need to keep track of any decisions made and any responsibilities assigned. Try choosing one person to take notes. Have that person project their notes on the screen so you can see the decisions and assignments recorded in real time.

If you follow these five rules, your next meeting (just like your next road trip) will be focused, fast, and maybe even fun!

8

Commonly Confused Words That Sound the Same

The English language contains commonly confused pairs of words that, when spoken aloud, sound almost identical to each other. It is easy to confuse their spellings and distinctly different meanings. Examples of such word pairs are *accept/except, stationary/stationery,* and *complement/compliment.*

Here are the words, their definitions, and an example sentence for each:

accept: (verb) to take something or agree to something
>   I *accepted* the job offer.

except: (preposition) other than
>   I told everyone *except* my boss.

stationary: (adjective) not moving
>   The sign looked *stationary,* but it actually revolved.

stationery: (noun) writing paper and envelopes
>   The *stationery* had our logo on it.

compliment: (verb or noun) a kind word spoken to another person

> He *complimented* me on my work performance. (verb)
>
> He gave me a *compliment*. (noun)

complement: (verb or noun) complete or go together well with something

> The shirt *complemented* the jacket.
>
> The lamp was a perfect *complement* for the sofa.

Tip: Since *compliment/complement* seem to cause the most difficulty, use this trick to remember the difference. *Compliment* includes the letter *i*. Remember this phrase: "When someone says something nice about me, *I* feel great!" *Complement* includes the letter *e*, which reminds us of the word *complete*. Remember this phrase: "*Complements complete* things."

How to Handle Criticism

When you receive critical or negative feedback, how do you respond? Are you comfortable accepting criticism even when you do not agree with it?

There are many ways to respond to criticism. You can argue. You can say nothing. You can accept the criticism and say "Thank you." Often the "thank you" option is the best. Here's why:

1. **If the person giving you the feedback does not have your best interest in mind, simply saying, "Thank you for the feedback" or "Thank you for the input," can help you avoid escalating the situation.** If you argue, you invite additional criticism.

2. **If the person does have your best interest in mind, saying "Thank you" will show that you are confident and can handle criticism well.** You will often gain the respect of the other person as a result.

3. **By choosing to accept criticism, you acknowledge that you are not perfect.** As a result, you may actually learn something new about yourself.

Simply accepting criticism without argument is not the only strategy to handle criticism, but very often it is the most effective strategy.

10

Command Attention Through Silence

Inexperienced public speakers often make the mistake of speaking before they are ready, beginning their presentations with an unimpressive "so," "um," or "okay, well." Create a polished and confident beginning to your speech with the use of a deliberate, 2-3 second silent pause before you speak. This pause will allow you to do the following:

1. Establish eye contact with your audience.

2. Assume a confident body stance.

3. Take control of the room.

Once you begin speaking, that brief pause will help ensure that your opening sentence stands out in a more dramatic way. Memorizing your opening phrase will further ensure a confident and successful beginning to your presentation.

11

The Presentation Strike Zone

Next time you watch a skilled presenter speak, pay attention to what the presenter does with his/her hands. You will notice that nearly all professional speakers keep at least one hand in front of their body while they speak, positioning the hand vertically between their shoulders and waist.

We call this the **Presentation Strike Zone**. (We created this term in 2006 while watching a baseball game and preparing for a presentation workshop!) If a presenter's hands are in the Strike Zone while she is speaking, you will be able to see her hands and face together at one glance. The hands and face (and voice) will appear to be in sync: as the presenter is speaking, her hands will subtly follow the intonation and flow of her voice. The result is that the presenter will appear focused, controlled, and powerful.

Next time you present, try to avoid speaking with both hands behind your back or at your sides. These postures appear weak or lifeless. Also, avoid crossing your arms, as this makes you look defensive or uncomfortable.

Instead, focus on keeping at least one hand in front of your body in the Presentation Strike Zone. If you need to gesture toward the screen or illustrate an important point with a big gesture, feel free to do so; just be sure to return your hand to the Strike Zone when you have finished your gesture.

12

How to Really Listen

There are so many things to think about when someone else is talking! It is incredibly easy to get distracted. If you don't train your brain to focus while you listen, you will never really hear what those around you have to say. This can lead to embarrassment ("I'm sorry, what was your name again?") and lost opportunities ("I don't remember hearing that the meeting was this afternoon...").

Here is how to train your brain to really listen:

1. **Listen to every word.** When someone is talking, pay attention to each and every word he or she says. It helps to repeat the words in your head while the person is speaking. This repetition will give your mind something to do and help you to stay focused.

2. **Focus on listening, not interpreting.** Instead of trying to summarize, paraphrase, analyze, or interpret what the other person is saying while you are listening, just listen. Imagine you are a voice recorder. Try to "record" the words rather than interpret them. Take notes, if appropriate.

3. Confirm before responding. When it is your turn to speak, first confirm your understanding, then comment.

These three steps help shift the focus from your inner thoughts to the words that the other person is saying. Try these three steps during your next conversation. You may be surprised by how much you have been missing!

13

Two Must-Haves for Every Effective Presentation

Some presentations are good; some presentations are bad. You can tell the good from the bad by answering two simple questions:

Question 1: In one sentence, what is the presentation's main message?

Example: This presentation explains that checking email and text messages during meetings negatively impacts workplace relationships and reduces productivity.

Question 2: In one sentence, what is the audience supposed to do with the information presented?

Example: The audience should stop checking email and text messages during meetings.

Good presentations have a focused message and an actionable outcome. As a result, they are highly effective. Bad presentations lack focus, an actionable outcome, or both. As a result, they are confusing and produce no results.

14

Project Confidence When Saying Your Own Name

Your name is important. How will people remember you if they don't know your name or cannot pronounce it correctly?

Ask yourself three questions:

1. **Do people understand your name the first time you say it?**

2. **Do people pronounce your name correctly?**

3. **Do people call you by the name you want to be called?**

Most of us have been living with the same name for decades. Our name is so familiar to us that we rarely give it much thought. For almost everyone we meet, however, our name is new information, and it can be difficult to understand.

Just like any new information, you need to present it clearly so that the listener can quickly and easily understand what you have said. When you say your name to someone for the first time, you need to do three things:

1. **Pause between your first name and last name:** "My name is *Allison* (pause) *Tubio.*" (**Not:** Allisontubio)

2. **Find the stressed syllables in your first name and last name.** Stretch and emphasize those syllables: "My name is *ALlison tuBIo.*"

3. **Tell the person what you would like to be called.** Say this clearly as well: "Please call me *Ali.*"

Practice: Look at yourself in the mirror. Say your name clearly. Say it again.

15

Acronyms and Initialisms

Many people in the business world love to use acronyms and initialisms. Acronyms are abbreviations made from the first letter of other words and pronounced as a word (SaaS, WIIFM, NASA). Initialisms are abbreviations made from the first letter of other words but pronounced as separate letters (UI, EOD, OOO). Although it may be tempting to use abbreviations like these, it can be a bad idea. Here are three reasons:

1. **Often the same few letters mean different things to different people.**

2. **If your audience (or reader) does not understand an acronym or initialism and they feel that they should, they may be too embarrassed to ask the meaning.** This can lead to misunderstandings.

3. **Even if your audience understands the acronym or initialism, it may take them a few seconds to recall the meaning.** In these few seconds, they may lose focus or stop listening to your presentation. If this happens multiple times, it can hurt the effectiveness of your presentation.

If you do decide to use acronyms or initialisms in your writing or presentations, remember to follow these rules:

Rule 1: Avoid using acronyms or initialisms in formal writing and presentations.

Rule 2: Avoid using acronyms or initialisms when speaking or writing to outsiders (people outside of your company, your team, and/or your industry). People outside of your company or industry are more likely to misunderstand the meaning of the acronym or initialism.

Rule 3: If you must use an acronym or initialism, always define it the first time you use it, unless it is universally understood by the general public. Ask yourself: Would your grandmother understand the acronym? If not, define it.

The potential misunderstandings that can result from the use of acronyms and initialisms greatly outweigh the benefits of using them. If you have to use them, use them with care!

16

Give Up Control for More Polite Communication

Polite communication is not just about word choice. Polite communication is about giving control to the listener. If you tell someone to do something, you maintain control. The result is an assertive and potentially aggressive statement. If, however, you ask someone to do something for you, you imply that they have the option to say "no." This choice is interpreted as politeness.

The following variations on the same basic request illustrate this control principle. The second example in each pair is in the more polite form because it relinquishes control to the listener:

> Please call Bill.
> Could you call Bill?

> I'd like you to move the meeting to Friday.
> Would you be able to move the meeting to Friday?

Different situations require different communication approaches. Sometimes you need to be direct or assertive.

However, when your goal is to be polite, remember to give the listener control.

Tip: You may be in authority over someone who would never think of saying "no" to you, but your effort to give them the perceived option to say "no" will be interpreted as politeness and respect.

17

Master Email Etiquette

When was the last time you reviewed your email writing practices?

Sending email is an automatic process for most of us: we do it so often and so quickly that it is easy to forget that there is a real person at the other end of the process! It is important to be efficient when writing email, but be careful that your "efficiency" doesn't damage your professional relationships.

Here are three email etiquette guidelines that can help you ensure that your email communications will be well received:

1. **Always start and end with a name.** Your emails should start with "Hello John" or "Hi Meg." Never skip the greeting or recipient's name unless you are writing to a large group of people or the email is part of an ongoing thread. Also, make sure you type your name at the end of all your emails. The auto-inserted email signature is not enough.

2. **Always be nice.** Never write angry emails. This is easy to fix: never write emails when you are angry. Starting your emails with a short greeting can soften the tone: "I hope

you are doing well" or "I hope you had a nice vacation" or "Thanks for your help with (recent project name)."

3. **Be timely and thorough.** Find out what your company and manager expect in terms of your email response time, and try to meet these expectations. At the very least, make sure you respond to all important emails within 24 hours. Also, if you receive an email with multiple questions or requests, make sure you respond to (or at least acknowledge) all of these questions/requests in your reply.

18

Who Is Responsible for Communication?

In a presentation, conversation, or meeting, who is responsible for making sure the key message is understood and the proper conclusion reached? Is it the speaker or the listener?

The answer depends on the culture.

Some cultures are **speaker-responsible**: the speaker is responsible for clearly explaining the message (or conclusion) to the listener/audience. There is a strong focus on "takeaways" and a clear explanation of "next steps." Also, interpretive phrases such as "what this means is…" are common.

Other cultures are **listener-responsible**: the listener is responsible for reaching the correct conclusion based on the information presented by the speaker. The speaker does not explicitly state the conclusion. Instead, the speaker presents the information, facts, and details that the listener will need to reach the proper conclusion on her own.

The US is generally considered to be a speaker-responsible culture. This impacts workplace communication in several important ways:

1. **The speaker often gives the reason or purpose for the conversation to make sure the message is clear:** "I am calling because..." or "I need the report by Friday so that..."

2. **Presenters are expected to clearly explain the structure and conclusion of their presentations.** In other words, the presenter/speaker is responsible for connecting the dots for their audience rather than relying on the audience to "figure out" the meaning.

3. **Meetings are expected to have a clearly-articulated purpose (agenda) and outcome (next steps).**

19

Clarify Your Points with Speech Capsules

Do you find yourself rambling on, unable to succinctly explain a key concept to a coworker or customer?

Try speaking in capsules. A **Speech Capsule** is a short, clear group of statements that begins with a topic sentence, ends with a summary statement, and lasts no longer than 90 seconds. It "encapsulates" the key ideas you want to express while preventing them from getting out of control.

Here is an example:

Question: What is the best way to find new customers?

Answer in a Speech Capsule: There are a few ways we can effectively find new customers (*topic sentence*). We could approach our partner network to see if they can make new introductions. We could contact our existing customers and ask for referrals. We could also try increasing our advertising budget. Of these three options, I think that asking for referrals is probably the best option, since our customers already understand the value of our services (*summary statement*).

Notice how the sentences in the Speech Capsule progress clearly and logically toward a clear conclusion. There are no long examples or stories about how each suggestion would work. There is no repetition or rehashing of the same ideas. There is a clear starting point, a clear ending point, and a set of clear ideas in the middle.

You can improve the clarity of your speech by trying to formulate your comments into capsules. Always begin with a topic statement. If you notice that you are rambling on, simply stop talking and wrap up your comment with a summary statement.

20

Quotation Marks with Commas, Periods, and Question Marks

Which of these sentences is correct?

A) She said, "I don't like ramen."

B) She said, "I don't like ramen".

Sentence A places the final period (.) inside the quotation marks. Sentence B places the final period outside the quotation marks. Sentence A is correct.

Here are the rules for using commas, periods, question marks, and other punctuation marks with quotations:

Commas (,) and periods (.) should be placed inside the quotation marks.

Our boss told us to wear our badges "at all times."

The manual says, "Wait five minutes before restarting the device," but I don't think that's necessary.

Question marks (?) follow these two rules:

A. If what you are quoting is a question, place the question mark inside the quotation marks:

> She asked me, "Have you ever seen this man?"

B. If what you are quoting is not a question, but your entire sentence is a question, place the question mark outside the quotation marks:

> Did they use the word "unicorn"?

Colons (:) and semicolons (;) should be placed outside the quotation marks.

> They had one "rule": be on time.

> The manual says, "Wait five minutes before restarting the device"; I don't think that's necessary.

Tip: If you are using a quotation mark to represent "inches," all punctuation marks should be placed after the inches mark:

> The screen was 15".

21

Magnetic Eyes Show Confidence

Eye contact matters. Good eye contact shows confidence (I believe in what I am saying!) and respect (I am listening carefully to what you are saying!). It helps to think of good eye contact like a strong Wi-Fi connection: it allows the uninterrupted flow of information from the speaker to the listener and back again. Breaking eye contact too frequently or avoiding eye contact altogether is like having a bad connection.

Making eye contact is uncomfortable for many people. If eye contact is difficult for you, try one of these tips:

1. **Look at just one eye.** Try focusing on the other person's left eye or right eye only. You can even switch eyes from time to time, if that is more comfortable for you. If looking at one eye is still uncomfortable for you, you can try looking at the top of the person's nose or the area between his or her eyes.

2. **Aim for 80%–not 100%–eye contact.** You should be looking at the other person's eyes for the majority of the

conversation. However, do not "lock" eyes with them or stare at them without blinking. This will freak them out.

3. **Imagine the other person's eyes are magnetic.** When you look away, imagine yourself being drawn back to their eyes. It is a good idea to break eye contact now and then. Just be sure you reconnect.

Tip: Eye contact has a strong cultural component. In many cultures, direct eye contact is a sign of confrontation and avoiding eye contact shows respect. If you work with colleagues from other countries, try not to interpret lack of eye contact as disrespectful. If you are new to the US, try to increase the amount of eye contact you make during conversations.

22

Small Talk Matters

You may ask yourself: Why should I bother with small talk? Isn't talking with others about such trivial subjects as the weather, traffic, or weekend plans a complete waste of time?

No. Small talk is essential to your success. Here's why:

There are two kinds of conversations: transactional conversations and relational conversations. A **transactional conversation** is used to complete a task: ordering food at a restaurant, requesting a task from a coworker, or asking for help. A **relational conversation** is not for completing a specific task. It is for building relationships.

Small talk is relational conversation.

Many cultures have regular (daily or weekly) activities that naturally build workplace relationships. (The frequent dinner parties in Japan and Korea are one example.) In the United States, other than the occasional holiday party or team-building event, these events are rare. In the United States, we use small talk to fill the gap.

By discussing our surroundings, our lives, our interests, and our plans, we learn about one another. We also start to find things we have in common with our coworkers. We start to trust our coworkers and they start to trust us. When we trust one another, we work better together: We collaborate. We ask for and accept help. We are more willing to overlook minor disagreements or mistakes.

Next time a coworker asks you about your weekend, take a few seconds to chat. That brief conversation may make the rest of the day much more productive.

23

I or Me?

Many people are rather confused these days about the correct use of the words *I* and *me*. They are confused about whether to say, "Mary and *I* are going to the store" or "Mary and *me* are going to the store." (*Mary and I* is correct in this sentence.) Use of the word *I* seems to be stuck in the "on" position. People seem to be positively afraid of ever saying "Mary and *me*," even when it would be correct. Here are guidelines for knowing when to choose *I* or *me*:

Use *I* when you are one of the subjects of the sentence.

Sean and *I* will organize the trip.

Use *me* when you are not one of the subjects of the sentence.

The boss took Megan and *me* out to lunch.

Dan sent the email to Amy and *me*.

Tip: If you are still confused, try the "preposition check." Look for the prepositions (words like *to, about, by, for,* etc.) in the sentence. These words must never be followed by the word *I*. For example, in the sentence, "The report was written *by* Kendra and *I*," you will notice that the word *by* is followed by *I*. This is incorrect. The correct sentence is, "The report was written *by* Kendra and *me*." This will not fix every *I/me* problem, but it is a great first step.

24

The Short-Answer, Long-Answer Response

When meeting with executives or other high-level decision-makers, it is important to get to the point quickly. This is especially true when you are responding to yes/no questions. The problem with yes/no questions is that they require yes/no, black-and-white answers. If you are not prepared for the question or if the answer is not black-and-white, this can be difficult. Next time you are in this situation, try the Short-Answer, Long-Answer Response.

The **Short-Answer, Long-Answer Response** begins with a very brief "yes" or "no" and then continues with a longer explanation or qualification of the short answer. This addresses the decision-maker's need for a simple, direct response, but it also gives you the chance to clarify, support, or qualify your response. Here are two examples:

Example 1 (A short answer followed by a long answer that qualifies the short answer):

> **Executive:** Do you expect your team will be able to finish the project by the deadline?

You: The quick answer is "Yes." That being said, there are several factors that could affect our ability to deliver on time, including changes to the specifications and unforeseen problems with the code. So while I am confident in our ability to deliver on time, it is possible the deadline could slip. I will keep you updated on any unforeseen delays.

Example 2 (A short answer followed by a long answer that supports the short answer):

Executive: Are you confident in the technical abilities of your team?

You: Yes. Our project lead has been working on similar software for more than eight years. She has put a development plan in place and has also paired experienced team members with less experienced team members to make sure we address any technical hurdles competently.

25

How to Use a Dash

The dash lives up to its name—it's really one of the more dashing forms of punctuation. It's the fun little mark that gives you permission to interrupt your line of thought, sometimes in an exciting way. Here are some ways to use a dash:

A dash replaces commas, parentheses, or colons.

American authors—Hemingway, Thoreau, and Twain—influenced his work.

A dash shows a sudden change of thought.

You deserve—and will receive—the same attention that we give our biggest clients.

A dash sets off a pronoun from the noun it references.

The company founder—she was the woman we admired.

A dash creates suspense or excitement in a sentence.

They have the feeling of—anticipation!

(If you know a bit about typography, you might know the dash by two names: *em dash* and *en dash*. The rules above explain how to use the *em dash*, the longer of the two.)

Tip: To create a dash using your keyboard, follow these steps: 1) Type your word and leave no space. 2) Type two hyphens and leave no space. 3) Type the second word. The computer will convert the two hyphens into a single long dash.

26

Soften Statements by Avoiding *You*

To politely communicate the need for improvement or a direct request, try to avoid using the word *you*. The word *you* can be interpreted as accusatory, aggressive, or overly direct, and it might cause the listener to feel unfairly singled out or under attack. Avoid using the word *you* by trying one of the following strategies:

Change the subject of the sentence to focus on the goal, outcome, or behavior.

Accusatory: You never proofread your reports, so there are a lot of mistakes.

More polite: Proofreading the reports will help eliminate mistakes.

Use an *if* statement and the passive form of the verb.

Accusatory: You never respond to my emails quickly enough.

More polite: It would be really helpful if your email responses could be sent more quickly.

Change *you* to *we*.

> **Overly direct:** You should dress more professionally in the workplace.

> **More polite:** We should all dress more professionally in the workplace.

Tip: Sometimes using the word you is unavoidable, but making an effort to avoid it can go a long way toward preserving your workplace relationships.

27

Avoid the Coffee Stain Problem When Presenting

Several years ago during a presentation seminar, one of the participants began her presentation like this:

"I am sure you noticed the coffee stain on my shirt. I am sorry about that. I spilled coffee on myself on my way here. Anyway, let's get started..."

No one in the seminar had noticed the coffee stain until she called our attention to it.

When presenting, try not to draw undue attention to problems, mistakes, or unexpected changes. If you don't draw attention to them, chances are the audience will hardly notice.

Here are other "coffee stain" phrases to avoid:

> I haven't had enough time to prepare for this.
>
> This isn't my presentation, so I don't know the slides very well.
>
> I didn't mean to click that slide.
>
> Ooops, I didn't mean to do that.
>
> Hold on a second. I need to look to see where I put my notes.
>
> Sorry, I'm not very good with this software.

28

It's or *Its*?

Do you ever ask yourself if you should use *it's* or *its*? It's (it is) easy to see why people confuse *it's* and *its*. In many words, an apostrophe (') followed by *s* indicates possession: *John's car*. However, the apostrophe in *it's* represents a contraction of the words *it* and *is*. The apostrophe takes the place of the missing *i* in *is*.

Its (no apostrophe) is a possessive pronoun just like *his, hers,* and *ours* and does not require an apostrophe to show possession.

Here are the rules:

It's (with an apostrophe) is the contraction for "it is" or "it has."

> *It's* easy for me to understand the speaker's point of view.
> (=It is easy for me to understand the speaker's point of view.)

Its (no apostrophe) is the possessive pronoun for "it" and means "belonging to it."

> The company is known for *its* excellent customer service.
> (=The company is known for the company's excellent customer service.)

Remember: *It's* is short for *it is*.

29

Is It Time for a Communication Reboot?

When we regularly interact with the same people every day—family members, coworkers, managers—we make assumptions about how they will react in different situations. Perhaps a manager always says "No" to our new ideas, a coworker always complains when we ask for help, or a partner always complains about the dishes. These assumptions affect our behavior: we avoid suggesting new ideas to our managers, we avoid asking our coworkers for help, and we avoid asking our partners for help in the kitchen. We simply stop communicating.

What if we took a moment and purged our communication assumptions? What if we approached each of these situations as if we were communicating for the first time?

Perhaps our partner would help with the dishes.

Perhaps our coworkers would be happy to help.

Perhaps our manager would like our ideas.

There is a lot to be gained—and very little to be lost—from giving communication a second chance.

Tip: Next time you find yourself avoiding someone, try a communication reboot. Approach the situation with a new attitude and without the burden of assumptions or past experiences. You may be surprised by the result.

30

Give to Get

In the US, we communicate like ping-pong players: we take turns. When someone gives us information, we naturally want to respond. Use this cultural characteristic to your advantage by first giving others the information you want from them in return. Give to get.

It works like this:

> If you want to know someone's name, introduce yourself first.

> If you want to know where someone works, tell them where you work first.

> If you want a business card, give one of your business cards first.

This principle works with behavior as well:

> If you want to shake hands, extend your hand first.

> If you want a smile, smile first.

> If you want kindness and respect, be kind and respectful first.

31

How to Use a Semicolon

Semicolons are not just for emoticons! They play an important role in grammar. The semicolon has two basic uses:

1. **You can use a semicolon to replace the period between two closely-related sentences.** Using a semicolon helps emphasize the connection between the two sentences.

   Examples:

   We provide an array of services. We have everything you need.
   We provide an array of services; we have everything you need.

   Ken is out of the office. He is attending an event in Asia.
   Ken is out of the office; he is attending an event in Asia.

   We had two hours. However, it was not enough time to finish.
   We had two hours; however, it was not enough time to finish.

   Amal can't attend. Therefore, we must reschedule the meeting.
   Amal can't attend; therefore, we must reschedule the meeting.

Tip: Notice that when a transition word (e.g., *however, therefore*) is used with a semicolon, it must be changed to lowercase and followed by a comma.

2. You can use a semicolon to connect items in a complex list or a list that already has punctuation.
In other words, a semicolon can replace a comma when a comma would be confusing.

Examples:

> Our services include the use of domestic, offshore, and nearshore investment vehicles; negotiations with domestic and international investors; and tax planning and regulatory compliance.

> I asked the supplier to provide a copy of the contract; a list including materials, costs, and expected delivery dates; and a completed W-9 form.

Tip: If you are not comfortable using semicolons, try doing some investigative reading first. Find an article in a newspaper or magazine. Highlight any semicolons you see. Ask yourself which of the above roles the semicolon is playing in each sentence.

32

Present Your Ideas Positively

Do you ever say things like, "I am not a good presenter," "I don't speak well," or "I am not good at (insert skill)" before you share an idea? Perhaps you do this to downplay your suggestion in case others don't like it.

When we put ourselves down, we limit our opportunities, weaken our language, and signal our unwillingness to learn or change. This can negatively impact how people perceive us and how we perceive ourselves.

From a communication standpoint, this can limit our ability to share our ideas and influence those around us. Take a look at these statements. Which is more powerful?

A) I am not really a creative person, but this is my idea for the presentation slide layout.

B) This is my idea for the presentation slide layout.

Clearly, B is the more powerful statement.

Consider these:

A) I know I'm not a great presenter, but I think that a shorter presentation would be more effective.

B) I think a shorter presentation would be more effective.

Statement A limits the speaker's influence over the situation. Statement B is more powerful.

Next time you share an idea or make a suggestion, make sure you don't start with a negative comment about yourself. Let the idea speak for itself.

33

So, Like, Um, Yeah, You Know

"So...some people use...um...you know...like...uh..a lot of... you know...filler words when they...um...speak."

The extra sounds or words that people add to their speech are sometimes called "filler words" or "speech noise." Some people also call them "credibility killers" because they make speakers appear unsure of their topic.

Filler words, when used excessively, are like static: they obscure the main message. Whenever possible, you should avoid using filler words. Replace them with a silent pause. Notice how clear the sentence above becomes when the filler words are removed:

_ Some people use _ a lot of _ filler words when they _ speak.

Most of us have a favorite filler word or two. The trick is to 1) discover which filler word is your favorite and 2) eliminate this word from your speech. Try these steps:

Step 1: Choose a topic.

Step 2: Use your smartphone to record yourself talking freely about the topic for two or three minutes.

Step 3: Review your recording. Write down any filler words or phrases you used. Keep track of how many times you used these words or phrases.

Step 4: Write your most commonly used filler word on a piece of paper. Put it where you will see it every day. Practice avoiding this word when you speak.

Step 5: Once a week, choose a new topic and record yourself again. Keep doing this until you can speak freely without using filler words.

Tip: If you speak another language fluently, be careful that filler words from your other language do not appear in your English.

34

Word Count and Culture

Do you talk too much or too little?

Word count in speech has deep cultural roots. Anthropologists have classified cultures as either low-context (the United States, for example) or high-context (Korea or Japan, for example). **Low-context cultures**, it is theorized, have a smaller amount of shared understanding (context), perhaps as a result of a shorter cultural history or greater diversity. **High-context cultures**, by contrast, have a larger amount of shared understanding (context).

This has important implications for communication. People from low-context cultures tend to use a lot more words to communicate and place a lower value on individual words. By contrast, people from high-context cultures tend to place a lot of value on individual words and use fewer of them.

This may explain why foreign-born professionals from high-context cultures sometimes complain that Americans talk too much. It may also explain why these same professionals are perceived by their American coworkers at times as "too quiet" or "not clear in their explanations."

Tip: Next time you are in a conversation with a colleague
from another culture, remember that word count is cultural.
If you are an American, try to focus your statements. If you
are from a high-context culture and working in America, try
adding a little more background to your explanations and
requests.

35

How to Use *Etc.* Correctly

The abbreviation *etc.* comes from the Latin "et cetera" and means "and other things." In informal or technical writing, *etc.* is used to suggest the logical continuation of a list.

This abbreviation should only be used for things, not people. (If you want to talk about people, use another Latin phrase, *et al.*)

Here are a few rules to follow when using *etc.*:

1. Put a comma before the abbreviation etc. and a period after it.

> **Correct:** He is responsible for purchasing pencils, paper, printer ink, binders, notebooks, etc.

2. Traditional rules tell us to put a comma after etc. when it appears in the middle of a sentence. However, the second comma is often left out in modern writing.

> **Traditional usage:** Notebooks, paper, pens, printer ink, binders, etc., all go in the left cabinet.
>
> **Modern usage:** Notebooks, paper, pens, printer ink, binders, etc. all go in the left cabinet.

3. Do not add an ellipsis (...) after *etc.*

Incorrect: He is responsible for purchasing pencils, paper, printer ink, binders, notebooks, etc...

4. If you use *etc.* at the end of a sentence, do not add a second period after *etc.*

Incorrect: He is responsible for purchasing pencils, paper, printer ink, binders, notebooks, etc..

5. If your list of items starts with "such as," "for example," or a similar phrase, do not use etc.

Correct: He is responsible for purchasing items such as pencils, paper, printer ink, binders, and notebooks.

Note: *Et cetera* is often mispronounced as "ex cetera." The correct pronunciation is "et cetera." Be sure to pronounce it with a *t* sound after the first *e*, not with an *x* sound.

36

Recover Quickly

Everyone makes mistakes, but when we make mistakes in front of a large audience or at a critical moment, such as during an important meeting or presentation, they can be quite embarrassing. The key to managing mistakes gracefully is recovering quickly. Get back on your feet as quickly as possible! This will help ensure that a small mistake doesn't become a catastrophe. Here are three tips to keep in mind:

1. **Refocus your attention on the audience.** You may have dropped your presentation notes or forgotten what you were going to say, but don't let that disrupt your focus. Try to quickly focus your attention back on your audience and away from yourself and your mistake.

2. **Resist the urge to draw attention to the mistake.** If you clicked too far forward on your slides, don't say "Oh, I'm on the wrong slide!" Instead, simply click back to the slide you need without saying anything. If it is not a big deal to you, it will not be a big deal to the audience.

3. **Recover.** Just keep going. In many cases (such as when you stumble over a word or sentence during a presentation), it is best to simply pretend that the

mistake didn't happen and continue on. If you feel that you absolutely must address the mistake (when you call someone by the wrong name, for example), acknowledge it quickly and with a matter-of-fact tone ("I apologize for getting your name wrong") and then keep going.

Mistakes will happen, but if you remain in control and recover quickly, you will be remembered for your confidence and control, not for your mistakes.

37

How to Avoid Talking Too Much

Do you feel that people sometimes stop listening to you? Do your listeners seem to "check out" in the middle of your conversations? If so, you may be talking too much.

Your coworkers may avoid talking to you if they feel that they can't escape from your conversations, and they may ignore some of your ideas if they feel that you are just repeating yourself. You can avoid over-talking and improve the quality of your workplace conversations by following these five tips:

1. **After you make a comment, be sure to ask a question to your listeners to engage them in the conversation.**

2. **Give no more than one example for each point you make.** If you stop speaking after making a point and the listener wants to know more, he or she will ask.

3. **Don't fill the silence.** This is especially important in group discussions. Some people need the silence to think, and others are waiting for a moment of silence to jump into the conversation.

4. Slow down. If you tend to speak quickly, slow down! By speaking more slowly, you will think more carefully about your words and will not need to say as much.

5. Avoid giving too many opinions. Stick to the facts and you will say less.

38

Two Kinds of Presentation Pauses

You can use brief pauses to focus the audience's attention on key information in your presentations. Here are two strategies you can try:

Anticipation Pause

By pausing before a key piece of information, you create a feeling of expectancy, excitement, or curiosity. We call this the **Anticipation Pause**. Here is an example:

> There is one problem facing the world today that is more urgent and more critical than any other problem we face *(Anticipation Pause):* too little water.

Much like the set up to a joke, the Anticipation Pause creates impact by first preparing the listener to hear something significant and then withholding that information for 1-2 seconds. In this example, the pause is placed before the key phrase, "too little water."

Contemplation Pause

By pausing after a key piece of information, you encourage the audience to spend time thinking about or contemplating what you have just said. We call this the **Contemplation Pause**. It is especially effective after a question that you want the audience to answer in their minds. Here is an example:

> As we have learned, water is a critical resource. Most of us use more than we need. My question is this: What is one change you can make in your daily life to help save this valuable resource? *(Contemplation Pause)*

By pausing after the question, you are showing your audience that you are serious. You really do want them to think about this question.

Tip: Use Anticipation Pauses at the beginning of your presentation to build excitement about your topic. Use Contemplation Pauses at the end of your presentation to encourage the audience members to deeply consider the relevance of your information to their work or lives.

39

Understand and Use Hyphens

A hyphen is a punctuation mark used to make connections at the word level. A hyphen is the length of one typed letter (-). While they look somewhat similar, the hyphen (-) and the dash (—) are quite different.

A hyphen is often used with compound nouns and compound verbs. (These are two or more words used together as a noun or verb, respectively.)

The *co-founders* of the *start-up* were aware of the problem.

I will log in to reconfirm your reservations and to *double-check* the spelling of your name.

Dictionaries sometimes disagree on which compound words should be hyphenated. For example, some dictionaries recommend not hyphenating "cofounder" and "startup." Other dictionaries recommend hyphenating not only these two words, but also "log-in" and "re-confirm."

A hyphen is used with compound adjectives. These are two or more words used together to modify a noun.

follow-up email

long-term relationship

a *forty-five-year-old* man

A hyphen connects letters to nouns and numbers to units of measurement.

Make a *U-turn* at the corner.

The *12-foot* ceiling made the office seem bigger.

A hyphen is used with prefixes to prevent misunderstandings.

Please *re-cover* the garbage can once you're finished using it. (It's not "recover.")

A hyphen is used in phone numbers.

My phone number is *555-123-4567*.

A "hanging" hyphen is used when more than one prefix shares a base word.

The *pre-* and *post-assessments* will be given in class.

Tip: Unlike a dash, a hyphen can be typed by simply pressing the hyphen key on your keyboard. Make sure there are no spaces before or after a hyphen.

40

How to Present to Executives

Typically when you present information, you have two options: you can start with the background information and build to the conclusion, or you can start with the conclusion and then support it with background details.

When presenting to executives or senior managers, you should start with the conclusion first. Here's why:

When senior leaders listen to a presentation, they usually want to know three things: What are you talking about? Why is it important? What do I need to do about it?

If you start your presentation with your conclusion first, you will answer these three questions in the first 30-60 seconds of your presentation. Then, having captured the attention of your executive audience and having addressed their most pressing concerns, you can proceed with additional background details, if necessary.

Executives commonly interrupt presenters to ask questions. If you lead with your conclusion, interruptions will not negatively impact your presentation because you will have already shared the most important information.

41

Avoid Misunderstandings Before They Happen

You may from time to time find yourself in the awkward situation of not fully understanding what a manager, client, or coworker is trying to tell you. It is not necessarily your fault when this happens: the speaker may not be speaking clearly. It is your fault, however, if you allow yourself to walk away from the conversation without first obtaining clarification about what was just said. You can avoid misunderstandings by using these four clarification skills: ask, repeat, rephrase, and reflect.

Ask

Ask follow-up questions to obtain more information when things are not clear.

> You touched on _____. Can you expand on that?
>
> Do you have an example you can show me?

Repeat

Repeat what you heard to make sure you heard correctly.

> Did you say _____?
>
> Let me just confirm what you want me to do. I need to _____.

Rephrase

Rephrase an unclear message using different words.

> When you said _____, did you mean _____?
>
> In summary, you would like me to _____. Is that correct?

Reflect

Reflect the speaker's emotions to show that you understand the real message.

> It sounds like you are worried you will not finish it in time.
>
> It seems that you are frustrated. Is there something I can do to help?

Tip: Being a good communicator is not always about what you say. It is sometimes about helping others clarify what they are trying to say.

42

Give Your Presentation Bookends

Sometimes the best way to finish a presentation or a speech is to finish where you start. You might give a surprising fact at the beginning to capture your audience's attention and then repeat the same fact at the end of your presentation. You might open your presentation with a question and withhold the answer until the end.

This is called **bookending.** Just as you can use two bookends to support a stack of books and hold them together, you can use a matching or connected introduction and conclusion to support your presentation and hold it together.

One of the most exciting ways to add bookends to your presentation is to split a story between your introduction and conclusion. Just follow these three steps:

Step 1: Write out the entire story. Make sure it is not too long, and make sure it is relevant to the topic you are presenting.

Step 2: Find the key transition point in the story. This is the point where the story captures the attention of the listener and makes her want to know what happens next.

Step 3: Split the story. Move the part of the story before the key transition to the introduction part of your presentation. Move the part after the transition to the end of your presentation. By only telling half of the story at the beginning of your presentation, you can create a feeling of anticipation. The audience will want to know what happens and will want to listen through to the end of your presentation to find out.

Bookending is a great way to capture and maintain your audience's attention during a presentation. It also reinforces your key points and ties your entire presentation together.

43

How to Soften a Question

Although clear communication is often achieved by eliminating unnecessary words, it is possible to take simplification too far. When asking a question or making a request, for example, simplifying your expressions too much can make them sound like commands. Instead of simplifying, try softening your questions and requests. Here are three strategies you can try:

Focus on the positive.

How long are you staying? (**Not:** When are you leaving?)

Are you feeling better? (**Not:** Are you still sick?)

Package your question in a phrase.

I was wondering if you were coming to the event. (**Not:** Are you coming to the event?)

Can you tell me how to access the new system? (**Not:** How do you access the new system?)

Add *would* or *could* to your question or request.

Would it be possible to get a copy of the report? (**Not:** Give me a copy of the report.)

Could you send me the latest version? (**Not:** Send me the latest version.)

Note: Avoid the phrases "Would you please..." and "Could you please..." Despite the addition of *would/could* and *please*, these phrases are often interpreted as commands and not polite requests.

44

Avoid Absolutes

"My coworker *never* helps out."

"My manager *always* asks me to stay late."

"There is *no* communication between our departments."

Most of us have used absolute statements like these at one time or another. An **absolute statement** is an expression that uses words like *always* and *never*, typically to express our frustration with a situation.

Absolute statements, even if technically true, can convey an unnecessary harshness that may offend your listener or reader. Absolute statements also diminish our expectations of positive change and shut down otherwise open conversations.

Try softening absolute statements through the use of qualifiers such as *slight, quite, little, very, rarely,* and *seldom.* By making statements less "absolute," you can introduce a bit of hope into a frustrating situation and maintain a more open dialogue.

Note how these qualifiers function as softeners in each of the following examples:

My coworker *never* helps me out.
My coworker *rarely* helps me out.

My manager *always* asks me to stay late.
My manager *frequently* asks me to stay late.

There is *no* communication between our departments.
There is *little* communication between our departments.

Tip: When you soften your statement, you are not just being polite, you are also leaving some wiggle room to preserve your own credibility. The use of a qualifier may help you avoid the embarrassment of having made an absolute statement that turned out to be wrong!

45

How to Use a Colon

The colon's use is fairly simple: it functions to introduce clarifying information about the sentence that immediately precedes it. (The sentence you just read both described and demonstrated how to use the colon!) It helps to think of the colon as "announcing" the information that follows. It is as if the colon is saying, "Here comes the important part!" The following rules provide more guidance:

A colon can introduce items that explain or amplify what was just said.

The attendees were given three food choices: steak, fish, or tofu.

A colon can connect two sentences when the second sentence explains the first.

The intern faced a dilemma: she could ignore his fame and talk to him as a colleague, or she could act like a fan and ask him for his autograph.

A colon also follows a formal opening salutation in a business letter.

Dear Mr. Smith:

To Whom It May Concern:

Note: Most style guides agree that simple lists of words following a colon should not be capitalized. ("I bought three items: butter, milk, and cheese.") However, when a colon is followed by a complete sentence, you have a choice: you can either capitalize the beginning of the sentence or leave it in lowercase. We typically do not capitalize unless we are using two or more complete sentences after the colon.

46

Acknowledge Beliefs and Perceptions

Your beliefs and perceptions are unique to you. Your coworkers may not share the same ideas about how the world works. This can result in disagreements and/or miscommunications.

By acknowledging that others may see things differently, however, and by adjusting your approach to accommodate these differences, you can overcome or eliminate many communication challenges.

Next time you experience a miscommunication or a disagreement, ask yourself these questions:

1. **What might be important to this person that is not important to me?**

2. **What might be bothering this person that is not bothering me?**

3. **What might be motivating this person that is not motivating me?**

4. **How might I change my approach to reflect these differences?**

Once you have considered these questions carefully, take another look at the situation. Consider whether changing your approach might eliminate the issue.

By thinking carefully about your beliefs and perceptions and considering the beliefs and perceptions of others, you may find an easier path forward.

47

How to Present Effectively from a Seated Position

Presenting while seated offers unique challenges to the presenter. Here are three tips to help you maximize audience engagement when you present from a seated position:

1. **Remove physical barriers.** Imagine that there is a straight line connecting you to your audience. If there is anything blocking the line, move it. Set your laptop to the side, uncross your arms, and remove any unnecessary equipment from the center of the table. You want a clear channel between you and your audience. This will reduce distractions, help your audience stay focused on you, and help you stay focused on your audience.

2. **Adjust your posture.** To captivate your audience from a seated position, you need to speak from a posture of authority. If possible, raise your chair. Sit on the front two-thirds of your chair and position both of your hands on the table, slightly apart. When you are speaking, lean slightly inward toward your audience.

3. Use the Presentation Strike Zone. Imagine a square drawn in front of your body from your chin to the table vertically and to the edges of your shoulders horizontally. This is the seated version of the Presentation Strike Zone (see page 21). You should keep both hands above the table and inside the Presentation Strike Zone when you present. This will allow your audience to see both your face and your hands at one glance and will help them stay focused on your presentation. On the rare occasion that you need to emphasize a particular point on your slides, reach outside the Strike Zone with one of your hands. Your audience's gaze will follow your hand and focus on the point in your slides that you are trying to emphasize.

48

Count to Five After Asking Questions

When you ask a question, do you stop and wait for others to respond, or do you continue to talk?

Take a look at this example:

> Since our current system for requesting paid time off (PTO) is complicated and expensive, we are planning to change the system. Before we start the vendor selection process, I wanted to hear from all of you. What changes would make the PTO system easier to use? I mean, maybe we could simplify the manager approval process. Or, maybe the user interface needs to be cleaner. Some people have complained that there are too many steps in the process. Do you think that is the main problem? What do you think? I was thinking that...

Notice that the speaker in this example continued talking after he asked his question. He should have stopped after "What changes would make the PTO system easier to use?"

To encourage input from others, try counting to five in your head after you ask a question. This will give others time to gather their thoughts and respond. The silence will feel uncomfortable the first few times, but resist the urge to keep talking or to answer your own question.

Try this:

> Since our current system for requesting paid time off (PTO) is complicated and expensive, we are planning to change the system. Before we start the vendor selection process, I wanted to hear from all of you. What changes would make the PTO system easier to use? *(Count to five slowly in your head: 1--- 2---3---4---5---)*

Tip: If you are meeting with an international group, this period of silence can be critical. Some cultures have a more structured, turn-based discussion style. Providing a few additional seconds of thinking time after you ask a question can help ensure you receive meaningful input from everyone.

49

How to Use *E.g.* and *I.e.* Correctly

These two Latin abbreviations are used to clarify information, but they are often misused:

e.g. = "exempli gratia" (for example)

i.e. = "id est" (that is/in other words)

E.g.

Use *e.g.* when introducing information that includes an example of what you are talking about.

> The CEO is considering new work policies, e.g., telecommuting and job-sharing, to help the company retain employees with small children.

> The CEO is considering new work policies (e.g., telecommuting and job-sharing) to help the company retain employees with small children.

In these examples, telecommuting and job-sharing are examples of the policies the CEO is considering. There could be more examples.

I.e.

Use *i.e.* when introducing information that renames exactly what you are talking about.

> The hotel will provide light refreshments, i.e., coffee, tea, and cookies.

> The hotel will provide light refreshments (i.e., coffee, tea, and cookies).

In these examples, the refreshments are exactly coffee, tea, and cookies.

Punctuation Note: As you can see from the examples above, *i.e.* and *e.g.* should be written in lowercase with periods after each letter. Most style guides suggest using a comma after the abbreviations. Do not italicize *i.e.* and *e.g.* unless the entire sentence is italicized.

Memory Tip:

Think of the *e* in *e.g.* as *example*.

Think of the *i* in *i.e.* as *in other words.*

50

When to Use *Save Draft*

Have you ever sent an email that you later regretted sending?

Emails are dangerous. They offer an element of anonymity that empowers us to say or write things that we would likely not say directly to the recipient in a face-to-face conversation.

For this reason, you should be extra careful when writing emails. Here are some guidelines that have helped our clients avoid problems in the past:

1. **Avoid writing emails when you are angry or frustrated.**

2. **If the topic of your email is sensitive, consider calling the person on the phone instead of sending an email.**

3. **After writing a sensitive email but before sending it, save a draft copy.** Give yourself an hour or so to clear your head and then reread your email. You may want to rewrite the email once your head has cleared.

Emails are forever. Once you send an email, you have no control over who reads it, and you cannot take it back.

Tip: Keep the To, CC, and BCC lines empty until you are confident that the email is appropriate. This extra step may save you from sending the email before you have had a chance to carefully consider its content.

51

Measure Actions, Not Confidence

How do you measure confidence?

Many of the people we train tell us that they lack confidence. We recommend that they focus on mastering a series of actions that help them appear and feel confident, rather than on trying to master confidence itself.

Confidence is intangible and perhaps impossible to measure. Actions are measurable.

In a meeting, for example, you can display confidence by performing these simple actions:

1. **Sit up and lean in, especially when you are speaking.** This will make you appear engaged and energetic.

2. **Keep your hands on the table and away from your face.** This will help you look and stay alert.

3. **Make frequent eye contact with the person who is speaking.** This will show that you are listening.

If you do these three things, you will look confident. Confidence itself is difficult to measure, but it is easy to measure whether you are (or are not) performing these actions.

52

Condense Your Message in a Pinch

Imagine this situation: You have been asked to give a presentation to senior business leaders at your company. You have been told to plan for 20 minutes plus time for questions. The future of your project depends on whether you can convince the business leadership that your project is important. You prepare your presentation slides. You practice for two weeks. The day of the meeting finally arrives.

When you walk into the room, your manager turns to you and says that due to time constraints, you will not be able to deliver your entire presentation. She asks you to give the group of business leaders just a quick, 60-second summary of your presentation. What do you do?

Don't panic. All you need to do is complete four sentences:

1. **Today, I am here to talk about** ___(Give the topic of your talk.)___.

2. **This is important because** ___(Explain how this topic impacts the business.)___.

3. The key things you need to know are ___(Give your three most important points.)___ .

4. What we would like to ask from you is ___(Tell the audience what you need from them or what they need to do. Be respectful.)___ .

Here is an example:

> *Today I am here to talk about* the new website development project. *This is important because* it impacts how our customers, vendors, and employees view our brand and can help or hurt our sales efforts. *The key things you need to know are as follows:* First, our current website is out of date and no longer accurately reflects our business. Second, we have selected a vendor to redevelop the site and have received a wireframe design proposal. Finally, with your approval of the design and the budget, we can move forward. The site can be launched in as little as three months. *What we would like from you* is input on the main design elements and approval of the proposed budget.
>
> I would be happy to go over additional details if you have questions. Thank you.

By summarizing key information succinctly, you will show that you know your topic and that you value your audience's time. If you do this well, you may find that your business leaders invite you to stay and deliver the original 20-minute presentation after all.

Index

Grammar and Writing

Acronyms and Initialisms........29

Commonly Confused Words That
Sound the Same......................15

How to Use a Colon...............89

How to Use a Dash 49

How to Use a Semicolon 61

How to Use *E.g.* and *I.e.*
Correctly.............................97

How to Use *Etc.* Correctly........69

I or *Me*? 45

It's or *Its*?............................55

Master Email Etiquette 33

Overcome Writer's Block
at Work 9

Quotation Marks with Commas,
Periods, and Question Marks 39

Understand and Use Hyphens ...77

When to Use *Save Draft* 99

Presentations and Public Speaking

Avoid the Coffee Stain Problem
When Presenting....................53

Clarify Your Points with Speech
Capsules 37

Command Attention Through
Silence..................................19

Condense Your Message
in a Pinch............................103

Count to Five After Asking
Questions.............................95

Effective Presentations Start
at Zero 7

Give Your Presentation
Bookends............................83

How to Present Effectively from a
Seated Position......................93

How to Present to Executives.....79

How to Sound Confident 3

Magnetic Eyes Show Confidence .41

Present Your Ideas Positively 63

The Presentation Strike Zone 21

Project Confidence When Saying
Your Own Name....................27

Recover Quickly......................71

Respond to Questions When You
Don't Have an Answer.............. 11

The Short-Answer, Long-Answer
Response............................ 47

So, Like, Um, Yeah, You Know..... 65

Two Kinds of Presentation
Pauses 75

Two Must-Haves for Every Effective
Presentation.......................... 25

Interpersonal Communication

Acknowledge Beliefs and
Perceptions............................91

Avoid Absolutes...................... 87

Avoid Misunderstandings Before
They Happen..........................81

Give to Get............................ 59

Give Up Control for More Polite
Communication 31

How to Avoid Talking
Too Much 73

How to Handle Criticism 17

How to Really Listen 23

How to Soften a Question......... 85

Is It Time for a Communication
Reboot? 57

Keep a Conversation Going.........5

Lead Effective Meetings 13

Measure Actions, Not
Confidence........................... 101

Set a Communication Goal
for the Next 52 Weeks.................1

Small Talk Matters.................. 43

Soften Statements by
Avoiding *You*..........................51

Who Is Responsible for
Communication? 35

Word Count and Culture 67

Made in the USA
San Bernardino, CA
23 January 2018